aveí bade ba de

Everybody Body

Hawai'i's Pidgin Poetry by

brada jó

Mutual Publishing

Library of Congress Catalog Card
Number: 2002108579

ISBN 1-56647-568-6
Design by Jane Hopkins
Cover photo by Tonya Yorke
All background photos © Douglas Peebles
All inset photos © Jozuf Hadley

First Printing, September 2002
1 2 3 4 5 6 7 8 9

Mutual Publishing
1215 Center Street, Suite 210
Honolulu, Hawaii 96816
Ph: (808) 732-1709
Fax: (808) 734-4094
e-mail: mutual@lava.net
www.mutualpublishing.com

Printed in Korea

Bradajo's approach to affixing language to the page remains unique among Pidgin authors. He sidesteps rules of orthography, syntax, and punctuation. Instead, his robust, good-humored calligraphic renderings of sound ripple across the white field, recreating the play and surprise of speech.

—Frank Stewart, Professor of English, University of Hawai'i, Editor of *Manoa*, a writer's journal

Many readers of local literature remember the groundbreaking book of Pidgin poems in the early 70s called CHALOOOKYU EENSAI...designed to look like a composition book filled with child-like scrawl that was nearly unintelligable. Reading it was like learning how to read: sounding out words, trying different pronunciations until, "aha!" you got it. Figuring out the poems were part of the fun, and when you figured them out, you just had to find someone to read them to.

—Darrell Lum, Bamboo Ridge Press

If you will allow

In surveying my calligraphy spread out before me on the floor, it suddenly became clear that the way it comes together for me—it's difference as compared to other writing in pidgin today—comes from a not entirely conscious urge to render in visual terms the lyric rhythm, the talkstory, the communion of spoken pidgin.

They're playful puzzles, if you will allow; configurations of phonetic frolic not related to English or any other language for that matter, that invite your creative participation. Sounding it out helps too.

Someone once said to me that he felt pidgin couldn't be written. And as I think about that again now, perhaps he meant that pidgin can't be standardized and fitted into an already existing system, being the living expression of a culture of soul. And how does one express that? By allowing it, right?

So I allow this. No matter what. Not just to be different, not just to be difficult for whatever reason, but simply to allow that inner leading...no matter what.

bradajo

April 2002

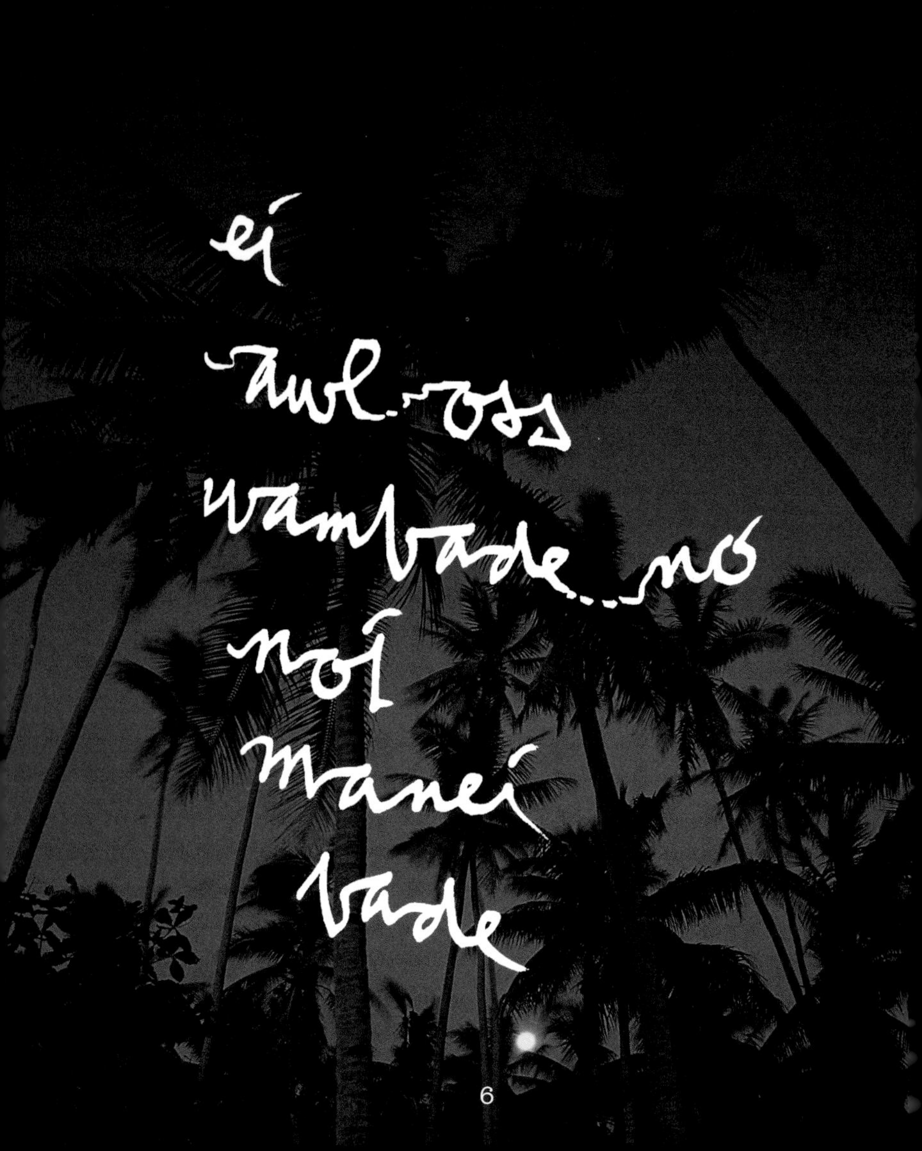
ei
awl-oss
wambade...no
noí
manei
bade

Hey! all us one body, no? not many bodies.

but, us no (don't) live 'um (it)!

eef awl oss
gaî conac shen
hah
dan gaî onei
waaambade no
awl oss
îugeda

If all us get (have) connection, huh? Then get (there is) only one body, no? All us together.

so
deis
avei
bade
bade
no

een..sai

so that's every body's body no? inside.

en
eef oss-goin
leee.. vom
hah
dan
oss..nogoin
hei.i
sombade
no

And, if us going (to) live 'um, huh?
Then us no going (to) hate somebody, no?

Us going live aloha (love) because
that's you're own body, no? you're making.

oss goin leev
aloha
bicos
dats yu own
bade no
yumeskin

When you hate somebody, huh?
you feel 'um inside your body, no?

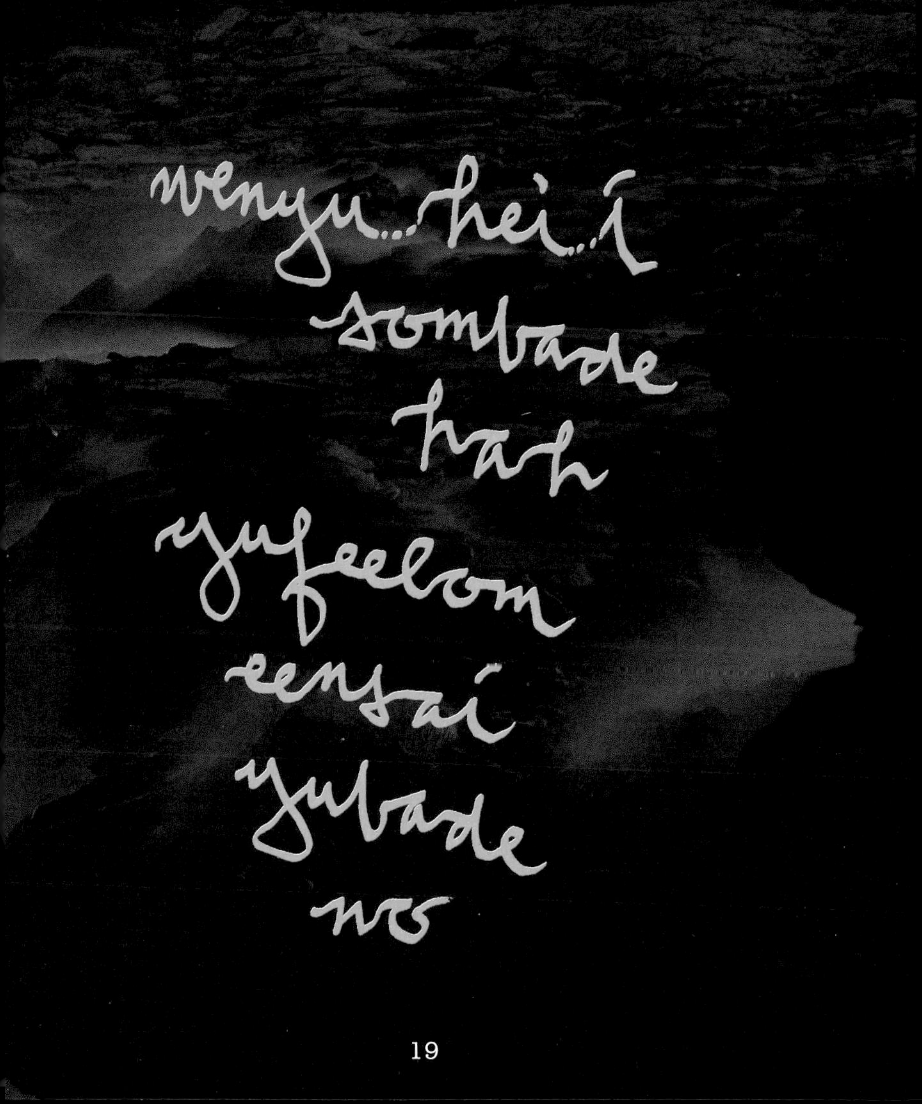
wenyu...hei...i
sombade
hah
yufeelom
eensai
yubade
nos

'jos...lícos
yunoseeda
conac
then

esnomeen
nomoa

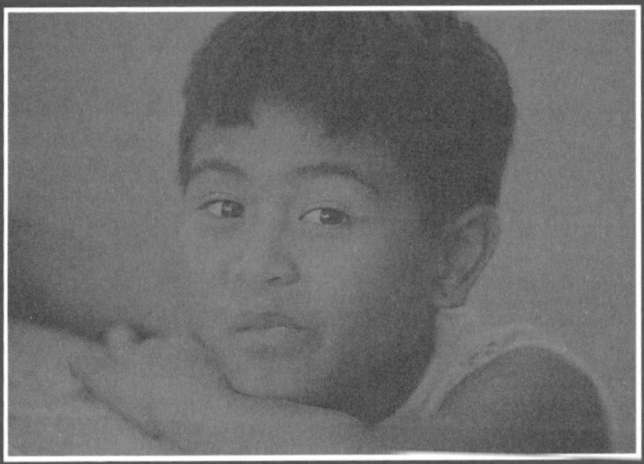

Just because you no see the connection,
that no mean (that doesn't mean) no more.

wenaluss
sombade... wawsín
hase
mía... lyk... tal
aloha... bicos
déis maí... badeno
atalín

When I look (at) somebody walking, huh? Me I like (to) tell aloha, because that's my body, no? I telling.

wai a
shoooden
aloha
awei
bade
ba

Why I shouldn't aloha everybody's body?

But, if my body (is a) different color from you body, or not, you figure your body (is) more better, because

yukalabade
sley-ohia
mo-lona
iyam

hah

Your color (of) body, stay (is) over here
more long time, huh?

danyufeega
yuzai agood
reezen
fohei i
mai bade
no

Then you figure you got good reason
for (to) hate my body, no?

But if get (there is) only one body, huh?

and everybody hate plenty other color body,
he going pile up, yuh? by and by,

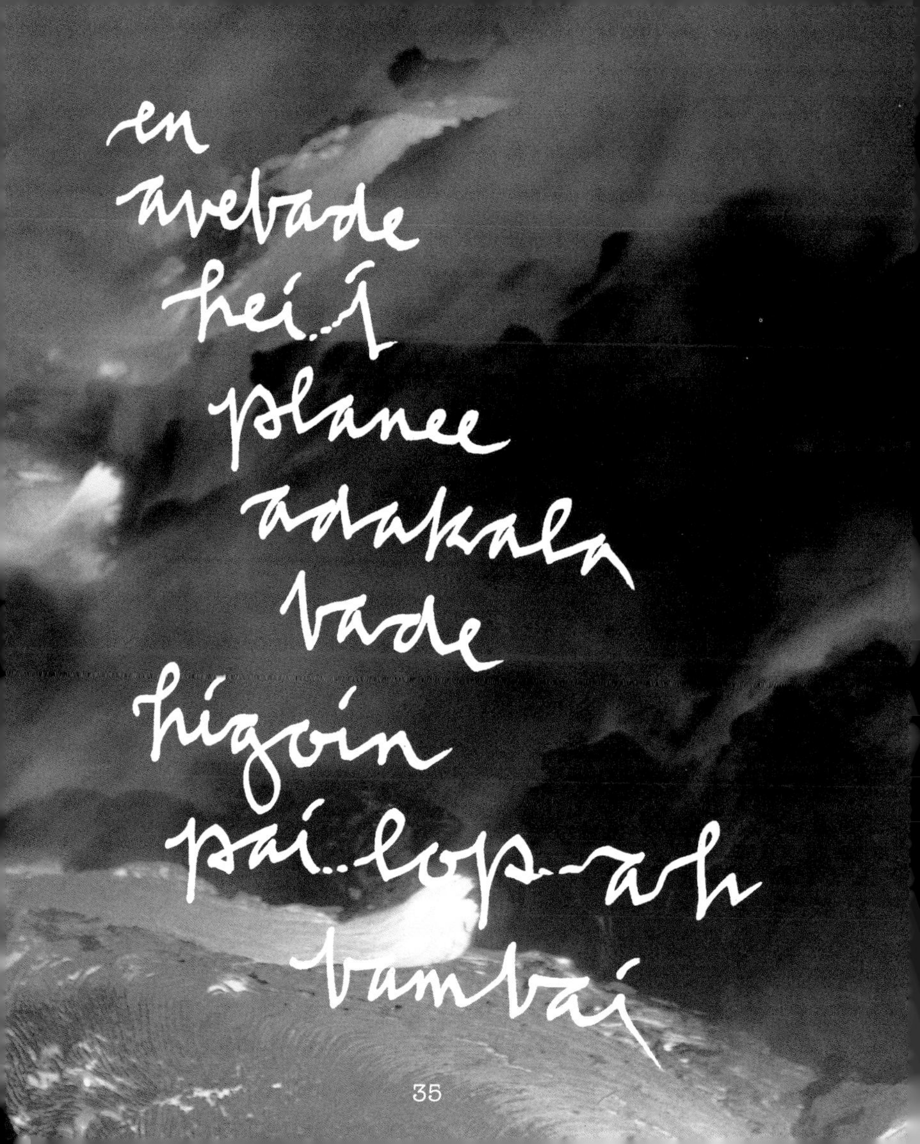
en
avebade
hei..j
planee
adakala
vade
higóin
paí..lop-ah
bambaí

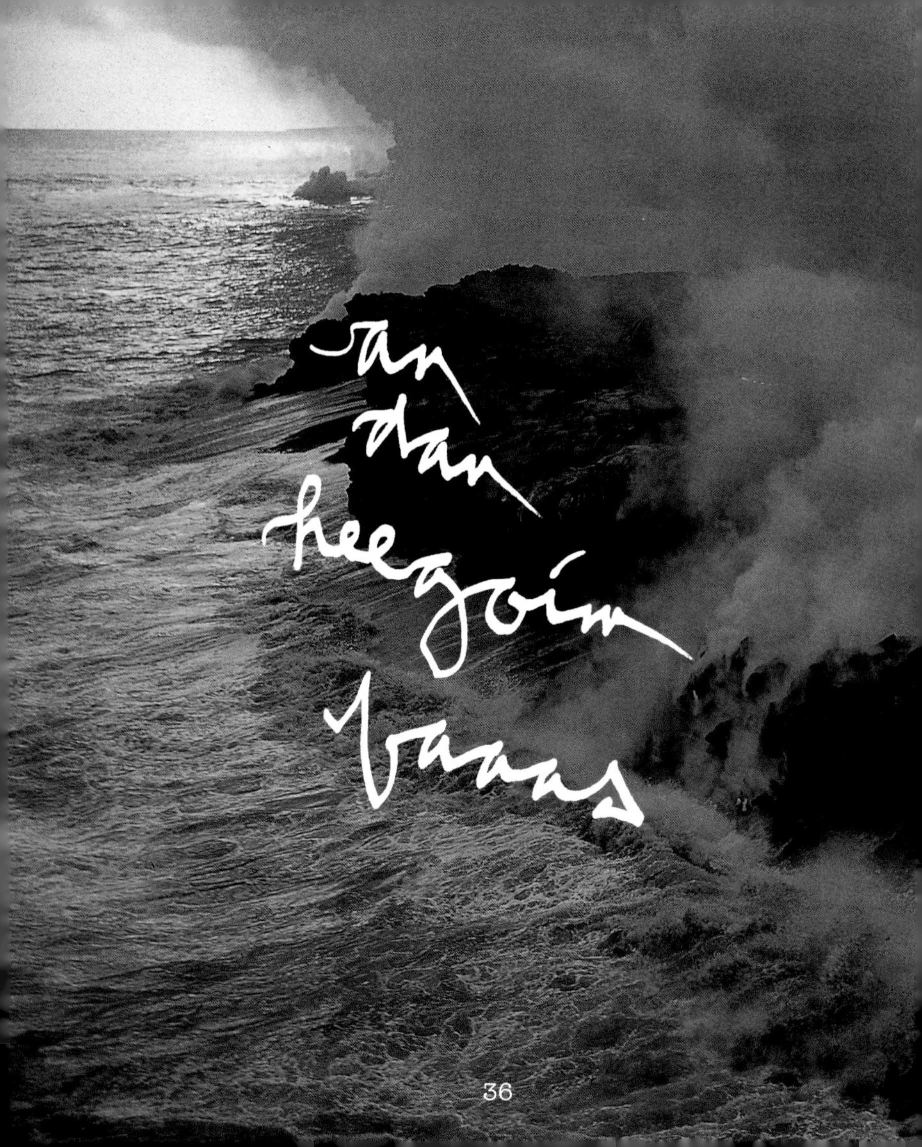
san dan hee goin baaas

and then he going bust!

wai.yuleenk
soplanee
brokembade
wendalu.lawa
peebaas
noo
yawk
sai

Why (do) you think (there were)
so plenty broken bodies when the two towers
he bust (they bust), New York side?

You think no more connection, or what?

seems to me, because everybody get (has)
different color body over here (in Hawai‘i),

sim
ly
me
vicos ravebade gai
deefeenz
kala
bade
ohiz

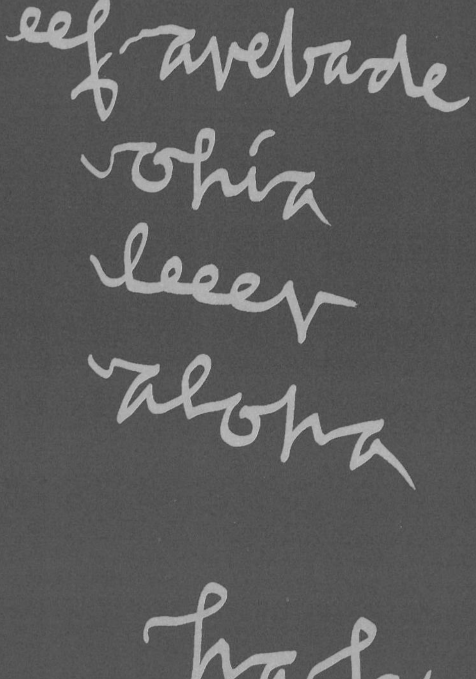

if everybody over here (in Hawai‘i) LIVES
aloha, huh?

us can start for (to) heal 'um everybody's body, if you like.

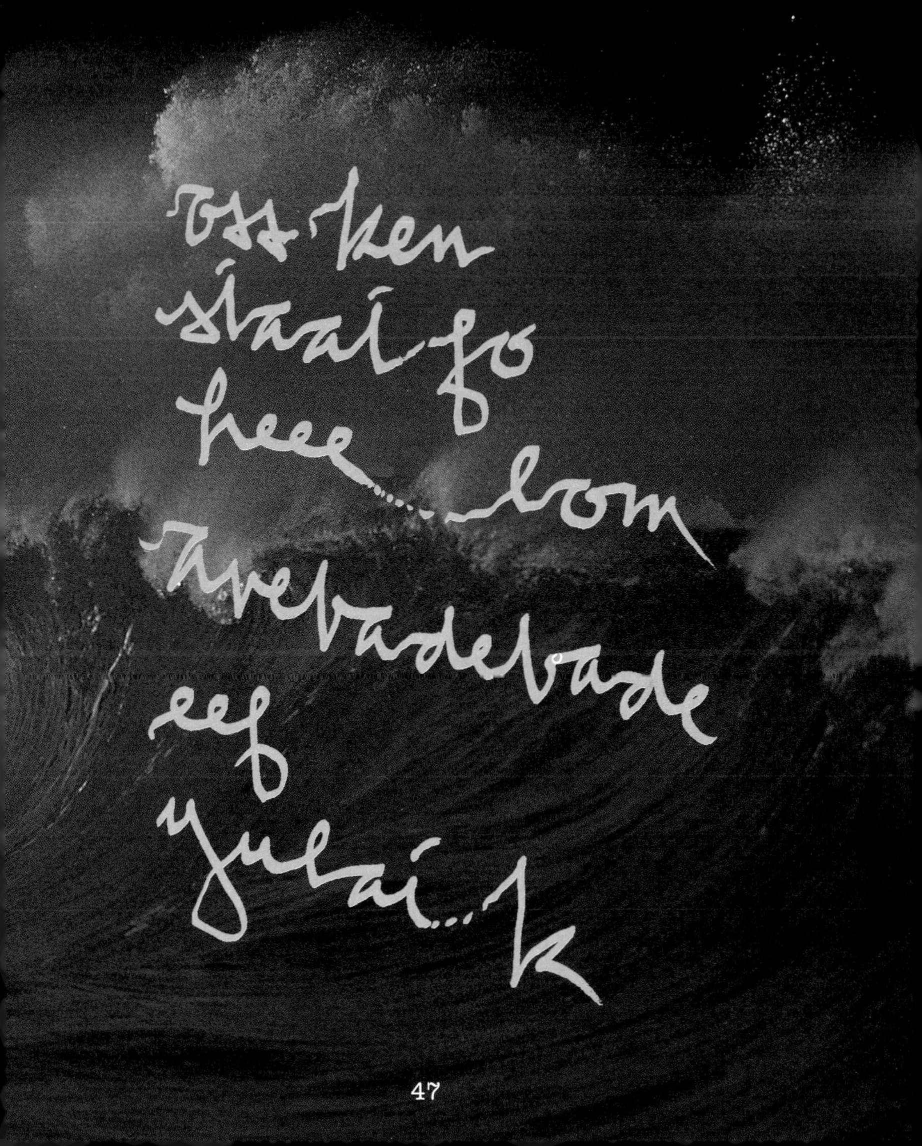

bachugada
leee...vom
da...aloha
noi...jos...poodom
da...sleeka
onlop
da
ka

But you gotta live 'um the aloha, not just put 'um the sticker on top the car.

Becuase, if nobody (is) going (to)
make more aloha body, huh?

vícos

eef...nobade
agoi...mek
moa
loha
bade

hah

hau
maach
moplanee
avebadebade
higoim
baas

how much more plenty everybody's body
he (is) going (to) bust!

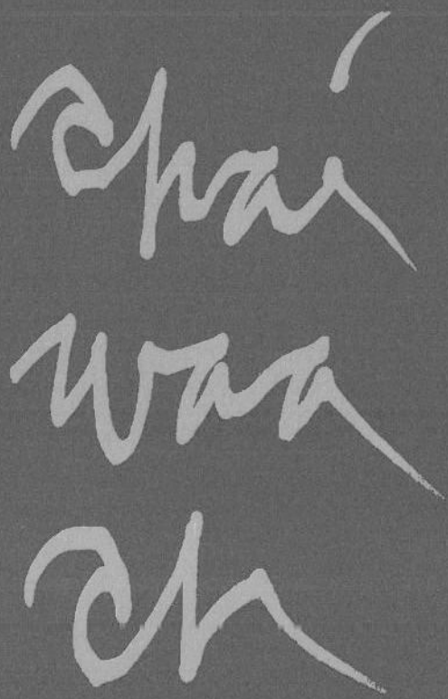

Try (and) watch.

How Avebade Bade Happened

It was soon after nine-eleven when a dear friend turned on me with riveting hatred. Avebade bade was my response to the recognition that we can choose to re-act or reverse that action. And what we choose to be adds to what we all be. Right? Yes, we ARE connected, though we've forgotten.

Hawai'i's tradition of sharing aloha—love—in spite of adversity, can bring this recognition of our oneness with each other to the point of critical mass, and thus transform the planet. This is our opportunity, multicultural Hawai'i!

In fact, it's already happening.

About the Author

Bradajo is a third generation kama'aina from Kaua'i...wait a minute! I don't know who I am. Really. I mean, I have past imagery that I can dwell on again, the same old stuff. Or, I can be presently conscious and be the Great Mystery of that. That's who and what I am (same as you), though I can't describe it other than to say it's the Greatest. It's only when I dwell on the same old imagery in that memory habit we practice, that I loose myself momentartily in my inventions. Anyway...